Jean Katz

Losing Norm

BOMBSHELTER PRESS
Los Angeles / 2012

ISBN: 978-0-941017-01-5

Bombshelter Press
www.bombshelterpress.com
books@bombshelterpress.com
PO Box 481266 Bicentennial Station
Los Angeles, California 90048 USA

Printed in the United States of America

Eulogy for Norm Katz by Rabbi Irving White, Ph.D.
Len Felder's Letter to Norm by Leonard Felder, Ph.D.

Cover photographs by Irv Moskovitz

Layout & design: Alan Berman

Dedication

Losing Norm *is dedicated to the memory of*
Norman Katz
Beloved husband, companion, lover, and friend
for 54 years

Contents

Introduction to *Losing Norm*

On October 20, 2008 my husband, Norman Katz, passed away after an eleven-month struggle with acute myeloid leukemia. We had been married for 54 years and best friends for 56.

During Norm's illness and during the mourning period after his death I wrote poems about my transition from wife of a vital, intelligent, kind, and loving man, to caretaker of an invalid, to partner in the hospice and dying process, and then to a grieving widow.

After reading Joan Didion's *The Year of Magical Thinking* I decided to honor Norm's memory by assembling my writings, a tribute letter from a friend, and a eulogy from another. Joan Didion's experience of loss was quite different from mine. John Gregory Dunne, her husband, died with no warning. She was in shock. Norm died after 11 months of leukemia and 20 years of heart disease and related emergencies. I was told, after the leukemia diagnosis, to be prepared to lose him within two months to two years. I hope this collection will help others who will experience their own passage of a loved one.

Near the end of Norm's life we received a remarkable letter from our friend, Dr. Leonard Felder, who had known Norm for just two years, yet understood him more deeply than some of his long-time friends. Lenny wanted Norm to read the letter while still alive, not wait to have the family read it after he had passed away. I also received copies of the other eulogies spoken at Norm's funeral. Excerpts from the eulogy delivered by Norm's long-time friend Rabbi Dr. Irving White are included here along with Dr. Felder's letter. I've also included a translation of the Kaddish prayer.

Everyone experiences the illness and loss of close family members and friends in different ways. Contemporary culture encourages people to remain brave and strong and *get on with normal life* as soon as possible. There seems to be insufficient acknowledgement of the physical and emotional reality of a long mourning period after a major loss.

In the Jewish tradition the deceased must be buried within 24 hours of death. Mourners are expected to shovel three scoops of soil over the casket at the burial, which takes place immediately after the funeral, to sit in their house and be cared for by family and friends for seven days, called *sitting shiva*, to say the ritual Kaddish prayer in the synagogue daily for a month, and then weekly for 11 months. The unveiling-the-stone ceremony at the end of 11 months signals the return to normal life. One can again wear bright clothes, listen to music, dance, and even remarry. I observed this yearlong process and found it to be healing beyond my expectation.

I pray that Norm's memory will always be a blessing for those who knew him or knew about him, and to those who will experience their own transitions, losses, and slow recovery.

Jean Katz, April 2010

New Country

On our 53rd wedding anniversary
we pedaled on a bike path
beside the Pacific,
the sun at our backs,
cumulus clouds floating
low in the blue sky.
Waves lapped the shore
as kids on roller blades
whizzed past us.

A month later we find ourselves
in a country called Leukemia
where a foreign language is spoken.
Vidaza, myeloid, corpuscular,
blastocyte, hemocrit roll off my tongue,
though I don't understand the words.

Old words mix with new:
prognosis, transfusion, infusion,
injection, cancer, relapse.
Days are consumed with counting:
white blood cells, hemoglobin,
number of platelets,
days of injections,
weeks from diagnosis,
weeks between treatments,
life expectancy.

I'm lost in the topography
of signs as well as words.
Is he breathing?
Is there color in his cheeks?
Can he walk a block?
Does he need a sudden nap?

Like an immigrant,
I long for the familiar tongue
of my old country with words like
bike rides, blue skies, clouds, waves,
hikes in the forest,
our 54th anniversary.

Swinging

It's Sunday.
I watch the acrobats
swing from ring to ring.
I hold my breath,
for fear that one might fall
without a safety net to catch him.

I am swinging
from a ring called despair
to one called hope
and back again.

It's Monday.
My husband returns from the hospital
where he had injections and blood tests.
"My hemoglobin count is still low," he says.
He bites into a turkey sandwich,
drinks a swig of iced tea,
then reaches for my hand.

"I'm glad you have friends," he says,
"and interests to keep you going.
I'm glad we have money in the bank
to take care of you.
I won't be here much longer."

"Norm," I say, "we don't know
how much time you have.
Give the treatment a chance."
I walk away, too choked up to say more.

It's Tuesday.
We go to a Chanukah party at an Ethiopian café.
Musicians play jazz from all over the world.
Candles burn in twenty menorahs.
People crowd around tables
heaped with potato pancakes and applesauce.

I chat with friends at one end of the room.
Norm greets friends at the other.
I look across

and notice he's dancing to the music.
Then I fall against a wall,
sobbing at the unexpected sight.

Friends surround me
until I'm able to dry my tears, straighten up
and walk across the room
to join him in the dance.

In the Pink

Norm stops every few steps
as he walks from the parking lot
to the entrance of the Griffith Observatory.
We'd promised our grandson this excursion,
and Norm insisted we go ahead with it.
I hurry inside to get a wheelchair.
Joshua and I take turns
pushing Norm from Pluto to Jupiter,
from Foucault's Pendulum to the Planetarium show.
He's happy when he sits,
but tired when he walks.
We ride elevators from floor to floor.
When we leave, Joshua wheels him to the car.
Unsteady, Norm stands,
then climbs into the passenger seat,
and I return the wheelchair.
His skin is somewhere between yellow and gray.

"Get your hemoglobin tested," I say.
"Not yet," he argues. "I want it to go up by itself."
This *push-resist* goes on for five days.
Finally he drives himself to the hospital.
The doctor calls for a transfusion.
Blood drips from a sack into his arm.
Six hours later Norm is home
carrying a bag of groceries.
His cheeks are pink.

Two Men

In the Land of Leukemia
I live with two men.
My husband and a stranger
inhabit the same fair skin.
Both have thin grey hair and hazel eyes.

One embraces me,
says, "I love you," often,
takes my car to get washed,
and, at night, when I've fallen
asleep over my book,
removes my glasses
and tucks me into bed.
We sleep so close that a thread
couldn't pass between us.

The other is a raging dragon.
Sparks shoot from his eyes.
Smoke plumes from his nose,
fire flares from his mouth,
all pointed at me.

After an eruption of rage
he falls, exhausted, to the couch,
then sleeps for three hours,
and returns to me as the man
who has held my hand
in the movies for 55 years.

A word from me
calls forth the dragon,
a word I can't predict.
In all the years together
I haven't yet mastered
the nuances of language needed now,
when to speak
and when to remain silent.

Bloodlines

Steady as the ticking of a clock,
one drop at a time,
blood trickles from the IV bag,
through a long tube
into my husband's arm.

Who was the angel
who donated this blood
so Norm can live?
A student from Compton,
a musician from El Monte,
a cab driver from Lawndale,
an immigrant from Nairobi?
And why did they do it?
To atone for a sin?
Out of gratitude for health?
Because it feels good to give?
Because they might
need it back one day?

People talk about blood family,
blood feuds, bloodlines,
fevers and ailments "in the blood."
What do they know?
When I look at this
sack of stranger's blood
I know we are all related.

We could survive on blood
donations from chimpanzees.
Palestinians could live
on transfusions from Israelis,
and Israelis from Palestinians.
Northern Irish and English
could transfuse each other,
and Greeks and Turks the same.

As soon as the blood stops dripping,
a nurse removes the tube,
Norm's lifeline.
She presses cotton and a Band-Aid

onto the bleeding spot,
then buttons the cuff of his shirt.

"Goodbye," she says.
"I'll see you next week."
"Goodbye," he says,
and takes my hand
as we walk past the tropical fish tank
to the elevator.

Len Felder's Letter to Norm

October 16, 2008

Dear Norman,

I decided to write you a note to tell you in print what I probably should tell you in person. Please forgive me for this, but I'll admit it's much easier getting mushy and personal in print than it is saying it in person.

I want to tell you how much I appreciate you and our friendship and who you are as a mensch. To fully understand why I appreciate you so much, there's a brief back-story. Twenty five years ago I was working for the National Conference of Christians and Jews, trying to help African-Americans in South Central. This African-American woman got in my face and said, "Lenny, we black folk don't need white folk coming in here with your white faces on your white horses trying to save us. Why don't you go try to fix the white males who run things. They're the ones who need to be saved and the rest of us (women and people of color) will be a lot better off if you focus your efforts on improving the way white men behave."

I took her seriously and I devoted the majority of my counseling practice and writing and speaking over the past 25 years to helping white males become more menschy and less insensitive. Essentially, I have been trying to get white men to be more like Norman Katz and I'd like to explain what I mean by that.

In the two years that we've been friends and having our great conversations I've found you are the best role model I've ever seen on several key factors that make for a true mensch. These are:

That men need to be less self-centered and they need to stretch sometimes out of respect for their loved ones. You do this so well. When I would watch you come to services just to be with your amazing wife Jean and when you would put up with theology talk that you don't enjoy just to be able to connect with Jean's passion and comfort, I said to myself, "That is the essence of what it means to stretch and go beyond your own comfort zone out of respect and love."

That men need to learn how to disagree without being disagreeable. I've found that in each conversation we've had about controversial issues, you have the ability to be respectful, kind, compassionate, and intelligent even when we are clearly disagreeing content-wise. This is a rare gift you have and you do it so naturally. You convey respect and warmth even while you clarify your opposition and your individuality. If only I could teach other men to be so gracious and not to revert to the male habits of sarcasm, one-up-man-ship, and shaming competitive comments.

That men need to learn how to balance knowledge about business and knowledge about emotions. This also seems to come naturally to you. You have a good head for business and worldly issues, yet you also have a deep awareness and appreciation of the inner life of emotions and vulnerability. This balance is so important and if men want to be as successful in life and in marriage as you are, they need to learn it.

That men need to learn how to laugh and have fun, rather than only focusing on survival. When I saw you and Jean on the bike path in Santa Monica and when I hear your stories about the enjoyable life you've built together, it makes me realize how much most men are missing out. You seem to get so much pleasure from your friendships, your extended family, your partnership with Jean, your professional life, your home life. And you clearly love to laugh. This kind of well-rounded life needs to be taught to all the men who are so out of balance.

That men need to be less sneaky or manipulative, and much more honest. I've always found, even now with your difficult medical situation, that you are able to be honest, compassionate, and genuine even when the truth is painful. You don't run away from the truth, rather you embrace it with an inner strength and a gentleness that allows you to be a terrific role model for the rest of us.

I salute you for who you are. I truly don't know if you were born this way or if you had to work hard to become this way. But in the two years that we've become friends, I've enjoyed every conversation with you.

With love,

Lenny

The Last Breath

Norm's life didn't end the way I had expected. Because he'd had six angioplasties, a triple bypass, and one heart attack over the past 25 years I imagined he would die of a heart attack before me. Sometimes I even thought he might succumb to a fit of rage when something frustrated him beyond endurance.

Eleven months before he died, when he was diagnosed with leukemia, I pictured a last hour when we would listen to a Bach fugue on the stereo and hold hands. We'd say, "I love you," to each other for the last time. I'd continue to hold his hand until his breathing stopped. Then I'd kiss him, cover him, and phone the mortuary.

Two nights before he died he wheezed and coughed so much that I couldn't sleep beside him anymore and had to move into the spare bedroom. When I heard him call my name through the baby monitor I'd plugged in next to him, I ran upstairs. There I found he'd fallen on the floor after he'd tried to go to the bathroom on his own. He couldn't move and I couldn't lift him. I phoned the hospice nurse, who advised me to call the paramedics. They came in five minutes. I felt reassured by those sturdy, competent young men who strode through the house, checked Norm's pulse and blood pressure, then picked him up like a small child and put him back in bed. I helped him change pajamas, gave him a cough-suppressant, covered him, kissed him, and went back to the other bedroom to sleep.

An hour later I heard a thud and he called my name again. I ran up and found him on the floor again, but this time his head was in a wastebasket. He'd fallen when he tried once more to go to the bathroom. I phoned the paramedics again. They came back to help us, ever patient and kind. As soon as they left I pushed chairs against Norm's side of the bed, climbed in beside him, and stayed awake, listening to him cough and wheeze. I didn't want him to try to get up a third time.

In the morning I phoned for a hospice nurse to come change his breathing medication, then phoned an agency to send a full-time attendant. At noon a woman named Gail arrived. Soon she had sponge-bathed him, changed his sweat-soaked pajamas and sheets, and arranged the pillows to make him more comfortable.

In the early afternoon the hospice nurse arrived. She listened to his heavy wheezing and coughing, and then gave him morphine, haldol, and methadone. He relaxed into a peaceful sleep. I collapsed onto the spare bed downstairs to take a nap.

When I awoke at 8:00 P.M. Gail was sitting in a rocking chair in our bedroom, watching the TV with soft audio. "Are you an angel sent to help us?" I asked. She just smiled and lifted her finger to her lips.

It turned out that she was an angel, the one who watched over Norm as he died. At 2:43 A.M. she came into the room where I was sleeping. She touched my shoulder. I startled, opened my eyes, and looked at her. She'd been sitting up with Norm all night. "I don't think he is breathing," she said. "You'd better check him."

I dashed upstairs and touched his chest. No rise and fall. I put a mirror under his nose and in front of his mouth. No mist collected. I touched his arms, thighs, legs, belly, all still warm, but not moving. His mouth was open, just as it had been when he was struggling to take in enough air.

I phoned the hospice again to send a nurse, this time to confirm that he was dead. An hour later she arrived, checked him, and wrote her report. "You should call the mortuary now," she said. "Ask them to send their staff to pick him up and prepare him for burial."

While we waited for the mortician's men, I told Gail, "Go downstairs to the den. Lie down and get some rest. I'll stay with Norm until the guys come."

I crawled into bed beside Norm's quiet body and pulled the covers over both of us. It felt so right to lie beside him. My hand reached out to touch and hold his. I dozed until the mortuary men arrived in their navy blue suits and ties.

When the doorbell rang I jumped out of bed, went down the stairs, and let them in. We sat at the dining room table where I began to tell them about how Norm died. One of them studied the art in our house while the other made notes of my answers to his questions.

"What happens next?" I asked.

"We're going to take Norm's body to Mt. Sinai now," he said.

"And then what will they do?"

"In the morning they will bathe him, dress him in a special white coat, kind of like a bathrobe. It's called a *kittle*. They will put a little cap called a *kippah* on his head, then the *talit*, a prayer shawl, over his shoulders. Next they'll place him in the plain pine coffin you ordered. You can phone them after 9:00 A.M. to arrange the day and time of the funeral. Will there be embalming?"

"No embalming," I said, "and no make-up." I paused. "May I stay with him?" I asked. "I want to ride in the hearse with his body. I'd also like to help bathe and dress him for the funeral."

"Sorry, Ma'am, we can't allow that," he said. "Mt. Sinai won't let women do that for men or men for women."

I wanted to scream at them, "What kind of crazy rule is that? That's outrageous. Do you mean to tell me that I could sleep and have sex with my husband for 54 years, but I can't bathe and dress him for burial?" But instead of screaming I just nodded, too tired to argue.

I led them upstairs to Norm's body. They wrapped him in a shroud, a large piece of white cloth that looked like a sheet. Before they closed up the shroud I kissed him one last time. One man carried him over his shoulder down the bedroom stairs, and placed his body on a gurney. I walked with them to the front door, touched Norm's shrouded body one last time, whispered goodbye, then watched as they wheeled him out and into the hearse that would carry him to the mortuary. As soon as they drove away I turned and walked into the kitchen to telephone our children and Norm's sisters.

At first I couldn't move. I sat with the family address book in front of me, but couldn't open it or turn the pages. I looked at Norm's empty chair at the kitchen table, stroked the wood where his arm rested two days before. Then I stood up, went to the cupboard for his favorite coffee cup, opened the fridge and took out two ice cubes to put in the cup, reached above the fridge for the bourbon bottle, took it down, opened it, and poured the golden liquid over the cubes. I took a sip, carried it back to the table, found our daughter's phone number in the address book, and dialed.

Excerpts from the Eulogy for Norman Katz

by Rabbi Irving White, Ph.D.
Mt. Sinai Mortuary, October 22, 2008

It is not an easy task to overcome emotion and sadness in talking about
Norman, a dear and close friend for nearly 40 years, but, more important,
a loving husband, father, and grandfather, as well as a human being whose
character was one that is admired by all. There may be some comfort in
knowing that Norm passed away in his sleep, comfortably, and without
fear of death, and in knowing that he no longer suffers.

For us whom he left behind, his passing must be looked at in the light
of the powerful memory he leaves behind, to Jean, his wife of over 54
years, his children, and to all of us who loved Norman and are blessed by
his legacy of honesty, integrity, loyalty, and courage.

Norm was a small town boy, born and raised in Janesville, Wisconsin,
one of only a few Jewish kids in his school from elementary through high
school. He carried the burden of the outsider throughout all those years,
despite a strong family with several relatives in town. He was the youngest
of four and the only boy. He played football and basketball, but
remembered being self-conscious that he was shorter than others on these
teams. How all this affected Norm, we don't know, but, however it did,
he more than made up for this sense of the outsider when he enrolled at
the University of Wisconsin and met his true love, Jean, whom he married
on a brief leave from the U.S. Army and soon after she graduated.
Together, they raised two children, their daughter, Lisa, and son, Dan.

Norm entered the scrap metal business, familiar to him from
childhood, after his two years in the army. He proved to be quite adept at
business. After Norm and Jean moved many times with promotions from
several companies, he was transferred to Chicago by an aluminum scrap
brokerage with worldwide connections. While Jean became used to
accommodating to new neighborhoods and even cultures, Norm dealt
with worldwide business contacts from Japan to Germany. Close to 40
years ago the family moved from Chicago to Los Angeles when Norm
joined with Ed Teller and Jake Farber to expand Teller Metal Co., a new
brokerage specializing in international scrap aluminum recycling.

His important volunteer work as a paraprofessional counselor at the
Southern California Counseling Center gave him immediate and deep
rewards. I know how dedicated he felt toward this newer aspect of his

interests, and I'm aware of what Norm meant to his colleagues there, and, of course, to his clients.

I spent many hours with Norm throughout the past 37 years, hours in friendship, hours in confrontation, hours in probing as well as two men can, the nature of who we are, what this world is about, and all the usual things that two buddies talk about, including the status of the various sports teams we followed, the latest deals we both got on our many trips to Costco, and, of course, about the world of finance, which was Norm's forte. Norm was a man who relished the here-and-now, the world that was presented to him in terms that he could grasp and confront. He wasn't a scientist. He wasn't an ideological empiricist who claimed that everything that exists can be counted. Nor did he believe in the spiritual force of religion. Rather, Norm was a realist of a very special kind. He believed in the truth of kindness, of close friendships, in the love of friends, and particularly his family. They represented the heart of his reality, the reality that was the essence of truth and character for him. He didn't need theological support for his very human values that he had incorporated from his years of relationships, from his small-town beginnings to the urban communities in which he later lived his adult life.

I want to conclude with this paraphrase of a quotation from the Talmudic tractate "Brachot" or "Blessings." The human soul is a tiny lamp from the Divine Torch. It is the vital spark of humanity's flame. We can say with full faith that this flame burns brightly within Norman Katz.

The Mourner's Kaddish

Magnified and sanctified
may His great Name be
in the world that He created
as He wills,
and may His kingdom come
in your lives and in your days
and in the lives of all the House of Israel,
swiftly and soon,
and say all *Amen!*

Amen!
May His great Name be blessed
always and forever!

Blessed
and praised
and glorified
and raised
and exalted
and honored
and uplifted
and lauded
be the Name of the Holy One
(He is Blessed!)
above all blessings
and hymns and praises and consolations
that are uttered in the world
and say all *Amen!*

May a great peace from Heaven—
and life!—
be upon us and upon all Israel,
and say all *Amen!*

May He who makes peace in His high places
make peace upon us and upon all Israel
and say all *Amen!*

Not There

It's dawn and
I'm half-awake.
I reach my hand
across the bed
to touch him.
He's not there.

I always liked early
morning love the best,
my favorite way
to start the day.
One summer I gave him a coffee cup
with "Make me late for breakfast,"
printed on it.
Now he's not there.

Last night as I stood at the sink,
I felt his hands
slide around my waist,
his belly press against my back.
I inhaled and turned around
but he wasn't there.

I walked to the table
to light the Sabbath candles,
then stopped.
I blew out the match,
picked up my plate
of chicken and broccoli
and carried it into the den
to watch the news.
Sabbath arrived without my help,
and without his.

I caressed the arm of the chair
where his hand used to rest,
took another bite of chicken,
and watched the evening news.

Like Challa Dough

When I bake challa
I mix the flour, water,
two eggs, salt, and yeast.
Then I knead the dough
into a sticky ball.
I set it aside to rise under a towel.
Two hours later I knead it again,
let it rise again,
and finally tear the ball apart
into three separate lumps.
The dough doesn't want to separate.
Molecules cling together until
I pull them apart hard enough
so they have no choice.
Then I shape each one
into a long rope,
pinch the three together at one end,
braid them, and press together
the opposite ends.
After the ropes are braided
I let the dough rise once more,
then bake it in the oven,
remove it to cool,
and slice the bread at our Sabbath dinner.
When I look at the slice,
there's no separation.
It is one smooth, golden piece.

Norm and I were like that bread,
separate, but so intertwined
one couldn't see the separation.
My niece said Norm-n-Jean
was one word.
In the wee hours of the morning,
my arms wrapped around the pillow,
I still feel the molecules of my body
reaching to reconnect with his,
like one twist of challa reconnects
with the others during baking,
to make a whole smooth loaf.

Dancing, Drumming, & Mourning

Eight women in sweat suits
line up before the mirror.
The dance teacher moves.
"Reach up," she says. "Shout yes!
Push out. Shout no!
Reach up. Shout yes!
Push out. Shout no!"
Now she has us move our feet.
 Step right to three o'clock.
 Step back to six o'clock.
 Step forward to 12 o'clock.
 One, two, three, four.
 Step left to nine o'clock.
 Step back to six o'clock.
 Step forward to 12 o'clock.
 One, two three, four.
 Turn around, circle round the room.
As she calls out, I move,
focused on the steps,
focused on the music,
feeling the rhythm,
punching out the anger,
stamping out the grief.

On another day
twelve novice drummers sit in a circle.
Eli brings twelve hand drums into the room.
I choose one that stands
from the floor to my waist,
lean it toward me,
and listen as he beats a rhythm:
One, one-two, one-two, one, one.
I repeat his rhythm.
He beats: one, two, three, four,
one-two, one-two, one-two, one-two.
I copy.
Kabalistic drumming he calls it.
"Listen," he says, "like *Sh'ma.*
Pay attention to the silence.
Feel it. Feel opposites,
like *gevurah* and *chesed,*

strength and compassion
Connect to your heartbeat.
Connect to each other.
Beat hard, hard as you can.
Brush softly, just enough for a tiny sound,
Like the *still, soft voice*."

Again, release for me.
I beat the anger,
physical as bone and muscle,
into the drum.
And the anger
that hides behind the grief,
the anger
that is deep within the mourning,
for a while disappears.

The Answer

Friends ask, "How ARE you?"
"In the morning," I say,
"I get myself out of bed
and walk three miles.
I eat breakfast, listen to NPR,
then make a to-do list for the day.
I pay bills, make phone calls,
send emails, write, cook, run errands,
attend meetings, join friends for dinner,
go to a film, a lecture, a concert.
Sometimes I even laugh.
Finally I fall into bed
and read a few pages—
my normal life."

I want to say, since Norm died
I feel like I have a 'phantom limb.'
The hand isn't there
to open jars for me.
I told Norm he had to live
one day longer than me
to open all the jars I can't open.
Now I have to use a rubber gripper
when a jar-top is stuck.
Norm always filled my car with gas.
Now I wear a special glove
to open the gas tank.
Last week I scolded
his picture on the wall.
"How could you leave me
to organize our finances
for tax time?
That was your job,
and you were good at it."

We always agreed that we needed
at least twelve hugs a day
for good health.
More are even better.
Now there are no more hugs.
Part of me is missing.

Packing His Clothes

As I pack my husband's clothes
for the thrift shop,
I sniff under the arms
to see if the scent of him lingers.
It doesn't.
Norm was so clean.
He tossed everything into the laundry
after he'd worn it once.

Not like me.
Mother taught me to wear each blouse
and shirt until the soil showed
so the fabric wouldn't wear out
from too much washing.
Norm and I were both Depression kids,
but his family was more optimistic than mine,
sure there would always be enough.
My mother saved string, rubber bands,
cut buttons off old clothes
before she tore them up for cleaning rags,
used backs of old envelopes for note-paper.
Grandpa pulled a child's wagon
to the produce warehouse
to bring back bruised fruit
for Grandma to trim and can for winter.
Grandpa, Grandma, Mother, Norm—
they're all gone now.

At last I find a large T-shirt
with the musky smell of his shaving lotion.
I hold it back to sleep in,
a last remnant to keep him near
when the thrift shop truck
carries the rest away.

The Last Orchid

My neighbor brought me
a white orchid
on the day of Norm's funeral.
It had sixteen blossoms,
some open, some still buds.
The buds opened, one at a time.
Then the older blossoms began to drop.
Now only one remains.
As soon as the last one drops,
I'll prune the stem
back to the fourth notch,
put the plant by a window
that gets light but no sun,
water it once a week,
and watch for a new branch
to grow and then bloom.
Orchids do that.

It makes me think about Norm,
cut from my life sixteen weeks ago.
I wonder if the Buddhists are right,
and he'll return soon in a new body.
I'll take a careful look
at the babies in the mall
to see if any have his broad shoulders,
his full lips, quick smile,
and his attentive hazel eyes.

And the Lord God fashioned the rib that He had taken from the man into a woman and He brought her to the man. Then the man said, "This one, at last, is bone of my bones and flesh of my flesh. This one shall be called Woman, for from man she was taken." Hence a man leaves his father and mother and clings to his wife, so that they become one flesh. Genesis 2:22–2:24

Flesh of My Flesh

We started out as strangers,
but after 56 years, after all the hugs,
the caresses, the intertwined fingers,
hands held in movies,
thighs touching under blankets
at football games,
arms around waists on walks,
bodies aligned like spoons in sleep,
lips and tongues pressed
and mingling in long kisses,
eyelashes brushing cheeks,
the coupling,
we became one flesh.

No one warned me that
mourning would be so physical,
that the hair on my arms,
pores on my cheeks,
muscles of my thighs, my toenails
would search to reconnect.
I should have known.
I read it every year
in the second verse of Genesis.

I shouldn't be surprised
that I miss his touch the most.
Humans touch first
in our mother's wombs,
then as we nurse
and are rocked to sleep in their arms.
We cling to our daddies too,
and are carried on their shoulders.
For a few brief years we

separate from our parents' bodies,
to stand and walk alone,
but soon cling to a boyfriend or girlfriend,
and then we marry,
once again joining flesh to flesh.

Norm's death was a jolt to my body,
parts torn asunder,
a void, once filled by touch.

Plum Tree in Blossom

Outside my front door
delicate petals open
on straight brown branches.
Bees visit each flower
while hummingbirds hover
and point their beaks
into the red-belled abutilon below.

Years ago I sat
on this same bench
by the same front window
after the children had gone to sleep.
I watched the buds open
while I carried on a silent dialogue
with a friend who had moved away.
I continued the conversation
that had sustained me
over the years.
Poetry emerged.
I felt her loss again,
as though a family member had died.

When she phoned this morning,
we were laughing in a minute
and telling stories we'd saved for one another.
I felt that familiar excitement
when I recognized in her voice
the echo of my own thoughts
and choice of words.

Last fall we thought
the plum tree was dead
when the leaves fell
and the branches appeared lifeless.
Today the plum tree's blossoms
fall near the base
or blow beyond view.
They remind me
that life renews itself
in ways I can't predict or control.

On nights like this . . .

when my skin remembers the touch of skin,
and my flesh the embrace of loving flesh,
I think about Harlow's rhesus monkeys,
separated from their mothers,
in their cages
at the University of Wisconsin.
Offered the choice of a wireframe mother
with a nipple providing unlimited milk,
or a terrycloth mother
that gave no milk,
only the comfort of soft warmth,
the babies chose the terrycloth.
Their need for physical contact
was stronger than their need for food.

In later experiments,
young monkeys who received milk and warmth
developed into normal adult monkeys.
Those with only milk from the wireframe mother,
and no cloth alternative,
became like psychotic, asocial children,
twirling, staring, self-mutilating,
and attacking each other.
Harlow called it the *social isolation effect*.

On nights like this,
when my skin remembers the touch of skin,
and my flesh the embrace of loving flesh,
I recall a life with many hugs every day
and nights of slumber while embracing.
I wonder what *social isolation effect*
Harlow would have found
if he had studied primates like me
who bond for life,
then lose their partner of 54 years
and his life-giving touch.

Embers

It is October.
She watches the leafy bonfire
burn down to a pile of grey ashes
over hidden, smoldering embers.

A small breeze
ignites a second blaze
which spreads
to nearby leaves and twigs,
then dies.

It is the second anniversary
of her husband's death.
She still carries embers of the passion
that sweetened their life together,
smoldering, fading,
almost disappearing.

An old friend comes to visit.
With a surprise touch
and a warm embrace,
like an autumn breeze,
he reignites the latent fire.
It spreads to her fingers
and curls her toes,
She thinks her hair
may burst into flames.

Then the flame
wanes again to hidden embers
while she hopes
for a second breeze to come
before the embers cool
and vanish
in a last puff of smoke.

Night Sounds

A squirrel races across the roof.
A mosquito whines in my ear.
A dog howls outside the window.
A baby cries in the apartment next door.
A neighbor's car roars down the street.
The walls creak as the house settles.
The heater turns itself on, hums,
turns itself off.
Silence.
A crash,
the tinkle of broken glass
at the intersection.
A siren swells and retreats.

A woman, alone in bed,
remembers when she cuddled
into her husband's arms,
tuned out the night sounds,
and fell asleep,
cocooned in his warmth.

Now she jumps up at every creak and squeak,
checks to see if the door is locked,
the garage door closed,
the security alarm set,
its tiny red light
beaming in the dark.

After Kaddish

One day the well of tears dried up.
No words of mourning
spilled over white pages.
No words at all.
I'd said Kaddish every day for a month,
then every week for eleven more.
On the anniversary of Norm's death
I drove to the cemetery alone,
put red-tipped yellow roses
in an urn by his grave,
sat on a nearby stone bench
and wrote a letter to him
until I had no more to say,
and ended it with *I miss you. I miss you.*

Planes droned overhead under puffy clouds.
A steady hum rose from the freeway below the hill.
I wandered around the cemetery,
reading the gravestones of his neighbors,
Russian and Persian names
with pictures on the stones,
then drove home to phone our friends of 40 years.
"Come to dinner. Let's remember Norm together.
Let's plan for the coming year."

The next morning I went to the synagogue,
said Kaddish for him for the last time until next year.
As I walked out the door
I felt as if weights had fallen from my shoulders.
I was lighter inside and out.

Then I bought a red silk blouse
with ruffles at the sleeves and collar,
crepe slacks for dancing,
rouge for my cheeks,
and sparkly shoes.

Now I scan crowds to see
who will join me
in a new *pas de deux*.

www.ingramcontent.com/pod-product-compliance
Lightning Source LLC
Chambersburg PA
CBHW051741040426
42447CB00008B/1256